C-Series
#1

DEBAJYOTI BHATTACHARJEE

DEDICATION

I Debajyoti Bhattacharjee presenting a self manual book for understanding the C Language for the users and students. My approach is to make the society eligible for understanding programming language on 21st century. I dedicate this book to my:

Mother: Manjushree Bhattacharjee

Brother: Nabarun Bhattacharjee & Nabajyoti Bhattacharjee

Acknowledgments

Today, most people don't need to know how a computer works. Most people can simply turn on a computer or a mobile phone and point at some little graphical object on the display, click a button or swipe a finger or two, and the computer does something. An example would be to get weather information from the net and display it. How to interact with a computer program is all the average person needs to know.

But, since you are going to learn how to write computer programs, you need to know a little bit about how a computer works. Your job will be to instruct the computer to do things.

Basically, writing *software* (computer programs) involves describing *processes*, *procedures*; it involves the authoring of *algorithms*. Computer programming involves developing lists of instructions - the *source code* representation of software The stuff that these instructions manipulate are different types of objects, e.g., numbers, words, images, sounds, etc... Creating a computer program can be like composing music, like designing a house, like creating lots of stuff. It has been argued that in its current state it is an *art*, not engineering.

A fair question you may have is "**Why should I learn how to program a computer?**"

An important reason to consider learning is that the concepts underlying this will be valuable to you, regardless of whether or not you go on to make a career out of it. One thing that you will learn quickly is that a computer is very dumb, but obedient. It does exactly what you tell it to do, which is not necessarily what you wanted. Programming will help you learn the importance of clarity of expression.

A deep understanding of programming, in particular the
      notions of successive decomposition as a mode of analysis
      and debugging of trial solutions, results in significant
      educational benefits in many domains of discourse,
      including those unrelated to computers and information
      technology per se.

                              (*Seymour Papert, in "Mindstorms"*)

      It has often been said that a person does not really
      understand something until he teaches it to someone else.
      Actually a person does not really understand something
      until after teaching it to a computer, i.e., express it
      as an algorithm."

      (*Donald Knuth, in "American Mathematical Monthly," 81*)

                ****

C-Series #1

1. What is C programming?

Ans:-C programming is a language of 3rd generation provides the basics of every future language. C language is also known by structured oriented programming language as C program is a top down or top to bottom approach language.

2. Difference between object oriented programming and structure oriented programming.

Ans:-The basic difference between them are as follows:-

i) Object oriented program provide 'class', Where as structure oriented program provide 'structure'.

ii) Object oriented program basically based on real world problems, where as structure oriented program is basically based on showing complex mathematical problems.

iii) Object oriented program has down to top approach, where as structure oriented program has top to down approach.

iv) Google Chrome is the best example of object oriented program, where as operating system windows 95, 98 are best example of 'c'.

Syntax =technique e.g-int a,b;	Variables=carry value; ;=end on terminate	Integer=those number have no decimal Floating point=those number have decimal

3.Data Type in C

In C programming there are four types of data are found:-

i) **Int**

Int is the short form of integer. In C integer provides a unique feature of maintaining data which are basically a numbers without any decimal places. Integer data can hold both positive and negative numbers.

For e.g. 1,-1 etc.

The syntax for declaring int data in C program,

Int a,b;

Where,

C Int is a data type

3   4

a,b are the variables

; means the terminating symbol

integer   floating

ii) **Float**

Float means the floating point numbers. In other words those numbers or data have a miracle form i.e. both number is integral and decimal part are in **C** language by using the data type **float**.

The syntax for floating point number is

float x,y,z;

$$\left.\begin{array}{l} \text{Or} \\ \text{float p:=3.14} \end{array}\right\} \quad \text{size=4bytes}$$

iii) Char

Char is the short form of character. Char is the most important data type in C language because it provides a space for character. Keyboard is the input device consists of various keys where each key according to any language is a character. Characters compose of various types Such as small alphabets, symbols, special, wide space, enter key etc.

The syntax for declaring character in C is

Char a,b

Where

'Char' is the data type

'a,b'   is   are variable which store only one character

For e.g. char a='a'; b='a';

Note

- The stored character must be quoted in single quotation.
- The size of char data type is 1 bytes.

iv) String

String means the group of characters. The group of characters may consist of digits, specials, alphabets, etc. string data type must be quoted in double quotation (" "). The syntax declaring string in C.

$$char\ a[20]$$

Where,

Char is a character data type

a [20] is the variable with specified range of 20 ,means it carry 20 symbols, digits,

Alphabets etc.

for e.g.- char a[s] ={"INDIA"};

4. What are variables?

Ans:-Variables means the literal values we declare during the beginning of programs. Variables are basically declares for storing them in C appropriate manner these variables are used for displaying the information related raw and facts and figures. The syntax for declaring variables is,

<data types> var1 var2;

Where,

<data types> here we type required data type according to the program.

Var1 var2 are the variables, where we store our data temporarily in memory,

Note: Range of int= -32767 to 32767

5. **SHORT NOTES:-**

- **Control string:**

    The control string is a symbol is used to identify the data type in C language. This unique feature is found in C language. The symbols consist of a special symbol & a single alphabet.

Data type	Control string
char	%c (mod c)
signed int	%d (mod d)
float	%f (mod f)
Long int	%ld (mod ld)
double	%lf (mod lf)
string	%s (mod s)
unsigned	%u (mod u)

    Note: modulus operator (mod)

- **Identifier:**

    Identifier is names that are given to various program elements such as variables, functions arrays. Identifier consists of letters &digits are any order except a first character must be a letter.

    The rules to construct identifiers are:-

i. Only alphabets, digits & underscores are permitted.

ii. An identifier cannot start with a digit.

iii. Identifiers are case sensitive i.e. uppercase & lowercase.

iv. The maximum length of an identifier is 32 characters.

- **Reserve word:-**

Reserve word is the essential part of a language definition. The meaning of these words has already been explained o the C compiler. Every reserve word has some special meaning in C, therefore these words are known by key word. Some of the reserve key words are int, float, unsigned, double, string, auto void return, while, for, do, switch, break, continue, register, static, if, as, go to, union, char, struct etc.

ISCII	ASCII
Indian	American standard code for information interchange

- **Flow Chart:-**

A flow chart is a pictorial algorithm that uses boxes of different shapes to denote different types of instructions. A flow chart acts as a road map for a programmer and guides the programmer how to go from starting point the final point while writing a computer program. It is very times consuming and laborious to draws with proper symbol especially for large and complex program.

The symbols used in flow chart are:-

i. Start\stop

ii. Processing

iii. Read/write

iv. Decision

v. Connector/arrow

vi.   Looping

Q.1 Draw a flow chart to read and display the sum of two numbers

Sol.

.<u>Algorithm</u>

Step-1: Ask to read a number

Step-2: Stores the numb

Step-3: Ask to read

Step-4: Stores the number in B

Step-5: Set C=A+B

Step-6: Print

Step-7: End

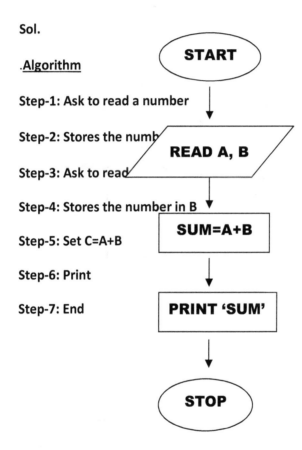

START

READ A, B

SUM=A+B

PRINT 'SUM'

STOP

Q.2 Draw a flow chart to print the simple interest.

Sol.

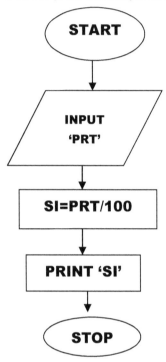

Q3. Draw a flow chart to print sum of nos. between one and enters number.

Sol.

Algorithm:

Step1: Ask to read a number.

Step2: Stores th

Step3: Set i=1

Step4: While

Step5: i<=N

Step6: i= i+1

Step7: Set sum = sum+i

Step8: Enel while

Step9: Prin

ep10: End

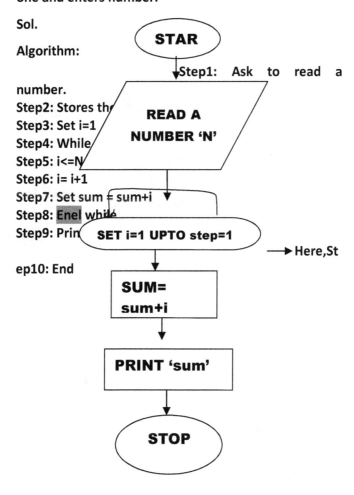

C-Series #1

Q.4 Draw a flow chart to calculate to determine whether the number is even or odd.

Sol.

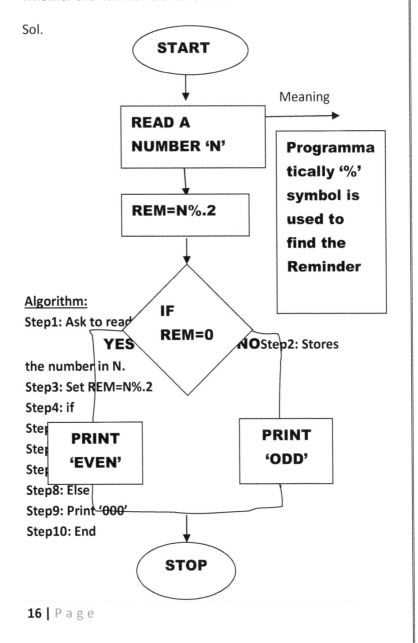

Meaning

Programmatically '%' symbol is used to find the Reminder

Algorithm:

Step1: Ask to read

Step2: Stores the number in N.

Step3: Set REM=N%.2

Step4: if

Step

Step

Step

Step8: Else

Step9: Print 'OOO'

Step10: End

Q5. Draw a flow chart to check whether the year is leap or not.

Sol.

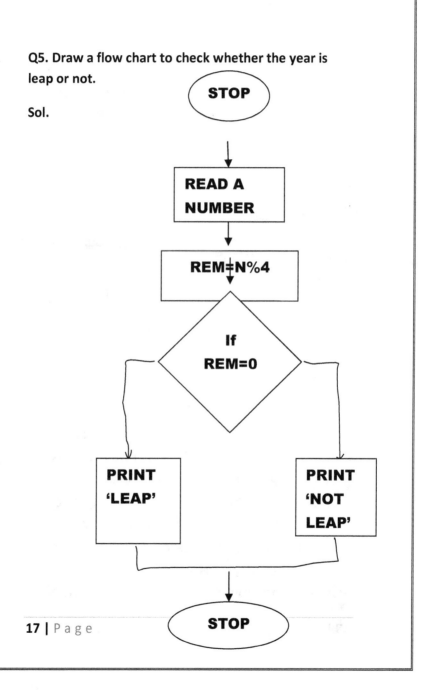

Q6. Define pseudo code and Algorithm.

Ans: Pseudo code derived from the word pseudo and code. Pseudo code is for detailed readable description of a computer program. Pseudo code generally consists of short English phrases to express a specific task.

The rules of pseudo code are reasonable forward. All statements showing dependency are to included. This include while, do, for, if etc.

> e.g.
> If rem is equal to 0
> Then
> Print even
> else
> Print odd

Algorithm is a sequence of instructions to solve a problem. Algorithm must be in a sequence i.e. Step wise. Algorithm uses a basic language to carry the problems until the desired result.

The algorithm prepared always before the flowchart and programs so as to understand the working of program. E.g. sum of two numbers.

Operators and Expressions:

1. What is operator?

Ans: C-operators are special symbols which instruct the compiler to perform mathematical or logical manipulations. Operators in C programs used to manipulate data and variables.

The classifications of operators in C are:-

i) Arithmetic Operators
ii) Relational Operators
iii) Logical Operators
iv) Assignment Operators
v) Increment and decrement Operators
vi) Conditional Operators
vii) Bitwise Operators
viii) Special Operators

Arithmetic Operators:

Arithmetic operators are used to solve mathematical operations like addition, subtraction, division, multiplication and reminder.

The arithmetic operators in C symbolically represented as

Name	Symbol	Operand 1	Operand 2	Result(int)
Addition	+	5	2	7
Substation	_	5	2	3
Multiplication	*	5	2	10
Division	/	5	2	2
Modulus	%	5	2	1

(in case of float – 2.5 is the result)

Relational operators:

These are used in C programs to compare the relationships between operators and bring out a decision according to the program. In C language, relational operators are used to check true or false result. These are six types –

Name	Symbol	Operand 1	Operand 2	Result
Equal	==	5	2	F
Not Equal	!=	5	2	T
Less then	<	5	2	F
Greater then	>	5	2	T
Less the equal	<=	5	2	F
Greater then equal	>=	5	2	T

Logical Operators:

Logical operators compare or evaluate logical and relational expressions. C language has three types of logical operators:-

a. **AND (&&) – ampersand:** The logical AND operators is used for evaluating two conditions or expression with relational operators simultaneously. If both the expressions of the logical operators are true then the whole compared expression is true.

b. **OR (||) pipe:** The logical OR is used to combine two expressions and the condition evaluates to true if any one of the two expressions is true.

c. **NOT (!):** The logical NOT operators takes single expression and evaluates to true. If the expression is false and evaluates to false if the expression is true.

Let operand 1 = 10 and operand 2= 20

Name	Symbol	Expression	Result
AND	&&	Operand 1<=10&&operand 2>=15	T
OR	||	Operand<=10||oprean d2>20	T
NOT	!	!(operand1>oprand2)	T
		!(operand1<oprand2)	F

Assignment Operator: (= symbol)

This evaluates the expression on the right of the operator and subtitles it to the value or variable on the left of the operand.

Result=oprand1+operand2

Increment and decrement operators:

There is one of the unary operators which are very useful in C language. The operators are ++ and --.

The unary operator can be used differently in the expression variables according to the nature of increment or decrement. For the variable, the nature of increment or decrement consists two types prefix operator and postfix operator.

e.g. ++i; ⟶ prefix operator i=5, ++5 result=6

(first increment then result)

i++; ⟶ postfix operator 5++, result=5 then increment

i+=2 or, i=i+2(increment by two step)

(i=i+ (1,2....) this is valid only for postfix i-c, i++)

Conditional Operator:

They consist of two symbols, the question mark (?) and the colon (:). It is also known by ternary operator. The expression in conditional evaluate true and false. Conditional operators evaluate only one expression.

Let, a=10, b=15

Syntax:-

Exp1? ee 1: re2

(a<b)? T=f

Eg. If (num%2==0); even: odd

C Language Program Structure:

1. **Write a C program to find the sum of two numbers.**
   Sol.

C-Series #1

```
#include<stdio.h>
#include<conio.h>
Void main ()
{
Int  a, b, c;  // deceleration of variables
printf("enter the 1st no=");
scanf("%d", &a);
printf("enter the 2nd no=");
scanf("%d",&b);
c=a+b;
printf("\n the sum is=%d",c);
getch();
}
```

Output:

Enter the 1st no= 5

Enter the 2nd no=5

The sum id=10

Expression:

\# --pre – processor (it links to the complier).

Include – it includes,

Stdio – Standard input and output

.h – Header file

( ) – Parenthesis	printf – Output
{ } – Braces	scanf – Input
{- Opening braces	\n – New line
} – Closing braces	\v – Vertical tab
\t – Horizontal tab	\a – Alert (bell)

// - Single line comment.

/* - Double line comment.

```
#include<stdio.h>
#include<conio.h>
void main ()
{
clrscr();  // clear screen
printf("hello world"); // output function
getch(); // to hold the screen
}
```

- **Write a C program to find the sum of three numbers and find the average.**

Sol.

```
#include<stdio.h>
#include<conio.h>
void main ()
{
int a, b, c, d;
float avg;
clrscr();
printf("\nenter the 1st number");
scanf ("%d",&a);
printf("\nenter the 2nd number");
sacnf("%d",&b);
printf("\nenter the 3rd number");
scanf("%d",&c);
d=a+b+c;
```

```
printf("\nsum=%d",d);
avg=d/3;
printf("\naverage=%5.2f",avg);
getch();
}
```

•

Sol.
```
#include<stdio.h>
#include<conio.h>
void main ()
{
int a, b, c;
float bill;
clrscr();
printf("\nenter previous reading");
scanf("%d",&a)
printf("\nenter the current reading");
scanf("%d",&b);
c=a-b;
printf("\nunit=%d",c)
printf("\nbill=%5.2",bill);
getch();
}
```

2. **Write a C program to find the multiplication of two numbers.**
   Sol.
```
#include<stdio.h>
#include<conio.h>
viod main ()
```

C-Series #1

```
{
int a,b,c;
clrscr();
printf("\nentee the 1st number");
scanf("%d",&a);
printf("\nenter the 2nd number");
scanf("%d",&b);
c=a*b;
printf(\nthe result is=%d",c);
getch();
}
```

3. **Write a C program to find simple interest.**

   Sol.

```
#include<stdio.h>
#include<conio.h>
void main ()
{
int p, r, t;
float si;
clrscr();
printf(\nenter principle amt.=");
scanf("%d",&p);
print("\nenter rate of int.=");
scanf("%d",&r);
printf("\nenter  time=");
scantf("%d",&t);
si=(p*r*t)/100;
printf("\n simple interest=%f",si);
getch();
}
```

4. **Write a program to print addition, subtraction, multiplication, division and modulus of two integers.**

Sol.

```c
#include<stdio.h>
#include<conio.h>
void main ()
{
int a, b, c, d, e;
float f, g;     // division, g – modulus
clrscr();
printf("\n enter 1st no");
scanf("%d",&a);
printf("\nenter 2nd no");
scanf("%d",b);
c=a+b;
printf("\n addition=%d",c)
d=a-b;
printf("\n substraction=%d",d);
e=a*b;
printf("\n multiplication=%d",e);
f=a/b;
printf("\n  division",f);
g=a%b;
printf("\n reminder=%d",g);
getch();
}
```

5. **Write a C program to swap.**

Sol.

```c
#include<stdio.h>
```

C-Series #1

```c
#include<conio.h>
void main ()
{
int a, b, temp;
printf("\n enter the two numbers a, b=");
scanf("%d%d",&a, &b);
temp=a;
a=b;
b=temp;
printf("\n a=%d",a);
printf("\n b=%d",b);
getch();
}
```

6. **Write a C program to read (scanf) three numbers display the total and average.**

Sol.

```c
#include<stdio.h>
#include<conio.h>
void main ()
{
int a, b, c, d;
float avg;
clrscr();
printf("\n enter the 1st number");
scanf("%d",&a);
printf("\n enter nd number");
scanf("%d",b);
prinf("\n enter the third number");
sacnf("%d",c);
d=a+b+c;
```

```
printf("\n total=%d",d);
avg=(a+b+c)/3;
printf("\n average=%5.2f",avg);
getch();
}
```

7. **Write a C program to solve the two expressions given below:**

Exp1: z=ax^2+bx+c

Exp2: z= (w + x)/y-z

Sol.

```
#include<stdio.h>
#include<conio.h>
void main ()
{
int a,b,c;
int x,z,w,y,z1;
clrscr();
Printf("\n enter the value a, b, c, x =");
scanf("%d%d%d%d",&a,&b,&c,&x);
printf("\n solving the expression\n");
z=a*x*x+b*x+c;
printf("%d*%d*%d+%d*%d+%d=%d",a,x,x,b,x,c,z);
printf("\nEnter The Values Of (w,x,y,z):");
scanf("%d%d%d%d",&w,&x,&y,&z);
z1=(w+x)/(y-z);
printf("(%d+%d)/(%d-%d)=%d",w,x,y,z,z1);
getch();
}
```

b) Z1= (w + x) / (y – z)

Sol.

```
#include<stdio.h>
#include<conio.h>
void  ()
{
int w,x,y,z;
float z1;
printf("\n enter the value of w,x,y,z=");
scanf("%d%d%d%d",&w,&x,&y,&z");
z1=(w+x)/(y-z);
printf("\n z1=%f",z1);
}
```

8. **Write a C program to find the area of** △

   Sol.

```
#include<stdio.h>
#include<conio.h>
void main()
{
int b,h;
float area;
printf("\n enter the value of base");
scanf("%d",&b);
printf(" \n enter the value of hight");
scanf("%d",&h);
ar=(b*h)/2;
printf("\n area of the triangle+%5.2",area);
getch();
}
```

△

9. **Write a program to find the area of a   using heroes formula.**

Sol.

```
#include<stdio.h>
#include<math.h>
#include<conio.h>
void main()
{
int a, b, c;
float s;
printf("\n enter the three sides of triangle a, b, c=");
scanf("%d%d%d",&a,&b,&c);
s=(a+b+c)/2
ar=sqrt(s*(s-a)*(s-b)*(s-c));
printf("\n the area of trigangle=%f",ar);
getch();
}
```

Library function of math.h:

#include<math.h>

Mathematical Notational	C – Function	Meaning
$\sqrt{x}$	Sqrt(x)	Find the square root of x
$|x|$	Tabs(x)	Find the absolute value of x
e^x	Exp(x)	Find the exponential of x
x^y	Dow(x, y)	The power of

		x is y
Log$^{(x)}$	Log(x)	To find the value of logarithm
Sin x	Cosec x	Sin (x)	Cosec(x)	To find the value of sin
Tan x	Cot x	Tan(x)	Cot(x)	To find the value of tan
Cos x	Sec x	Cos(x)	Sec(x)	To find the value of cos

10. Write a C program to convert the below seconds into number of days, hours, minutes.
    31558150 seconds.
    Sol.

```
#include<stdio.h>
#include<conio.h>
void main()
{
float min, days, hours;
min=31558150/60;
hr=min/(60*60);
day=he/(60*60*24);
printf("\nminutes=%f",min);
printf("\nhours=%f",hr);
printf("\ndays=%f",day)
getch();
}
```

11. Write a C program to convert the temperature from Fahrenheit to Celsius.
    Sol.

C-Series #1

```
#include<stdio.h>
#include<conio.h>
void main()
{
float c,f;
printf("\n enter fahrenheit=")
sacnf("%f",&f)
c=(5*(f-32))/9;
printf("\n celsius=%f",c);
getch();
}
```

12. **Write a C program to find the compound interest**
   (c i)
   Sol.

```
#include<stdio.h>
#include<conio.h>
#include<math.h>
Void main ()
{
Float p, r, n, ci;
Printf("\n enter the value of principal=");
Scanf("%f",&p);
Printf("\n enter the value of rate");
Scanf("%f",&r);
Printf("\n enter the time");
Sacnf("%f",n);
Ci=p*(pow(1+10/100,n))-p;
Printf("\n compound interest is=%f",ci);
Getch();
}
```

CI=P'

SI=PF

C-Series #1

1. **Write a C program to find whether a** **is scalene, isosceles on equilateral.**

   Sol.

```
#include<stdio.h>
#include<conio.h>
void main ()
{
int a, b, c;
printf("\n enter three sides of a triangle=");
scanf("%d%d%d",&a, &b ,&c");
if(a==b)
{
printf("\n equilateral triangle=");
else
printf("\n isosceles triangle");
}
else if(a!=b)
{
if(a==c)
printf("\n isosceles triangle");
else
printf("\n scalene triangle");
}
else
prinf("\n invalid side");
getch();
}
```

2. **Write a C program to find whether the is rectangle or not.**

   sol.

```
#include<stdio.h>
include<conio.h>
void main ()
{
int 90⁰, 45⁰, 45⁰;
```

```c
int a, b, c;
printf{"\n enter the angles of a rectangle=");
scanf("%d%d%d",&a &b&c);
if(a==90||b==90||c==90||)
{
if((a==45&&c==45)||(a==45&&c==45)||(a==45&&b
==45))
printf("\n rectangle");
else
printf("\n not a rectangle");
}
else
printf("\n invalid angle");
getch();
}
```

3. **Write a C program to read marks of four subjects then calculate total and percentage. Check what is the grade using below condition:-**

$$\geq 60 - A, \geq 45 < 60 - B$$
$$\geq 30 \text{ and } < 45 - c$$
$$< 30 - fail$$

Sol.
```
#include<stdio.h>
include<conio.h>
```

```
void main ()
{
float a, b, c, d, total, percentage;
printf("\n enter the marks of four different
subjects=");
sacnf("%f%f%f%f",&a,&b,&c,&c,&d);
toal=a+b++c+d;
printf("\n total of all subjects=%f",total);
percentage=(total/4);
printf("\n percentage of all
subjects=%f",percentage");
if(percentage>=60)
printf("\n grade a");
else
if(percentage>=45&&percentage<60)
printf("\n grade b);
else
if(percentage>=30&&percentage<45);
printf("\n grade c");
else
printf("\n fail");
getch();
}
```

4. **Write a C program to find the ASCII code to a given
   character**
   =>ASCII code for A to Z is 65 to 90
   ASCII code for a to z is 97 to 122
   ASCII code for 0 to 9 is 48 to 57
   Sol.
   #include<stdio.h>

C-Series #1

```
#include<conio.h>
void main ()
{
int val1,val2;
cha a, b;
printf("\n 1 ASCII ti character \n 2 character to
ASCII");
printf("\nenter our option=:");
scanf("%d",&val1);
if (val1==1)
{
printf("\n enter ASCII value (0-225):");
scanf("%d",&val2);
a=val2;
printf("\n character:%c",a);
}
if(val1==2)
{
printf("\nenter any keyboard character:");
scanf("%c",2b);
val1=b
printf("\n ASCII value of character:%d",val2);
}
else
prinf("\n enter valid choice");
getch();
}
```

Q. What is switch statement?

Ans: Switch statement refers to a break statement
on which the value of a variable or an expression

execute. The switch statement is a newer form of nested if statement. The following rules for switch statement that are used are as follows: -

    i.   The braces can be omitted when there is only one statement available in the statement block.

    ii.   The break statement is used to transfer the central to the end of switch statement,

    iii.   The default block either must be with the case labels.

    iv.   The default block is optional as this is similar to else statements.

The syntax for switch statement

<u>Switch (condition or expression)</u>

{

Case<label1>: statement;

      Break;

Case<lebel2>: statement;

      Break;

 Case<label n>: statement;

      Break;

 Default: statement;

}

1. **Write a C program to check whether a number is even or odd using switch.**

   Sol.

C-Series #1

```c
#include<stdio.h>
#include<conio.h>
void main ()
{
int a;
clrscr();
printf("\n enter any number");
scanf("%d",&a);
switch(a%2)
{
case1:printf("\n odd number");
break;
case0:printf("\n even number");
break;
default:printf("\n invalid");
}
getch();
}
```

2. **Write a C program to find the value of y using the given expression**
   When,

N=1	y=x+1
N=2	y=1+x/n
N=3	$y=1+x^2$
Default y=1+nx	

Sol.

```c
#include<stdio.h>
#include<conio.h>
void main ()
{
```

C-Series #1

```c
float x, y;
int n;
clrscr();
printf("\n enter the value of n and x=");
scanf("%f%f",&x, &y);
switch (n)
{
case1: y=x+1;
        printf("\n y=%f",y);
        break;
case2: y=1+x/y;
        printf("\n y=%f",y);
        break;
case3: y=1+x²;
        printf("\n y=%f",y);
        break;
default: y=1+nx;
        printf("\n y=%f",y);
}
getch();
}
```

3. **The frequency of a vibrating string which depends on length 'l' and linear clarity is**
   given by –

$$n = \frac{k}{l}\sqrt{\frac{t}{m}}$$

Where K is constant.

Write a C program to find when l=50,60, 70 and 80 cm

Sol.

C-Series #1

```c
#include<stdio.h>
#include<conio.h>
void main ()
{
float n, k, t m;
int l;
printf("\n enter the value of k, t, m,l=");
scanf("%f%f%f%d",&k&t&m&l);
switch(l)
{
case50: n=(k/l)*sqrt(t/m);
break;
case60: n=(k/l)*sqrt(t/m);
break;
case70: n=(k/l)*sqrt(t/m);
break;
case80: n=(k/l)*sqrt(t/l);
break;
default: printf ("\n invalid value of length");
}
printf("\n n=%f",n);
getch();
}
```

4. **Write a C program that will read the value of x and evaluate the function**

$$Y(x) = x^2 + 2x - 10, \text{ if } x < 10$$
$$Y(x) = |x|, \text{ if } x < 0 \text{ using switch statement}$$

Sol.

```c
#include<stdio.h>
#include<conio.h>
```

C-Series #1

```c
void main ()
{
float x, y;
clrscr();
printf("\n enter the value of x=");
scanf("%f%f%",&x, &y);
switch((x<0||(x>0&&x<10))
{
case0: y=pow(x,2)+2*x-10;
break;
case1: y=pow(x,2)+2*x-10;
break;
case3: y=pow(x,2)+2*x-10;
case4: y=pow(x,2)+2*x-10;
break;
case5: y=pow(x,2)+2*x-10;
break;
case6: y=pow(x,2)+2*x-10;
break;
case7: y=pow(x,2)+2*x-10;
break;
case8: y=pow(x,2)+2*x-10;
break;
case9: y=pow(x,2)+2*x-10;
break;
default: y=tabs(x);
printf("\n y=%f",y);
}
getch();
}
```

5. Write a C program to calculate the commission of a sale even considering their regions x, y and z displaying on the sales amount as follows: -

    i. For area code X;

S.A (sales amount)	com.
<1000	10%
<5000	12%
>=5000	15%

    ii. For area code y:

SA	com.
<1500	10%
<7000	12%
>=7000	15%

    iii. For area code Z

SA	com
<1200	10%
<6500	12%
>=6500	15%

Sol.

```c
#include<stdio.h>
#include<conio.h>
void main ()
{
float sa1, sa2, sa3;
float tot1, tot2, tot3;
float gt;
clrscr();
printf("\n enter the value if sales amount of 3 area=");
scanf("%f%f%f%f%f%f%f",&sa1, &sa2, &sa3, &tot1,
tot2, &tot3, &gt);
```

C-Series #1

```
printf("\n calculate the commission for area x=");
if (sa<1000)
tot=(sa1+10)/10;
if(sa1>=1000&&sa<5000)
tot1=(sa1+12)/100;
if(sa1>=5000)
tot=sa1*15)/100;
printf("\n commission for area code x=%f",tot1);
printf("/n calculating the commission for area code
y=);
if (sa2<1500)
tot2=(sa2*10)/100
if(sa2<7000)
tot2=(sa2*1)/100;
if(sa2>=7000)
tot2(sa2*15)/100;
printf("\n commission for area code y=%f",tot2);
prinf("\n commission for area code z");
if(sa3>1200)
tot3=(sa3*10)/100;
if(sa3<6500)
tot3(sa*12)/100;
if(sa3>=6500)
tot3(sa3*15)/100;
printf("\n commission for area code z=%f",tot3);
gt=tot1+tot2+tot3;
printf("\n grand total of commission=%f"/gt);
getch();
}
```
(: is used only for input and output)

Understanding the loop control structure (unit iii – 2nd position)

1. What is loop?

Ans: Loop control is used to execute and repeat a block of statement depending on the value of a condition. In C, there are three types of loop control structure: -

      i. For statement or for loop (entry loop)

      ii. While statement or while loop. (entry loop)

      iii. Do while statement or do – while loop. (exit control loop)

Structure for loop

For (initialization; condition – test; increment/decrement)

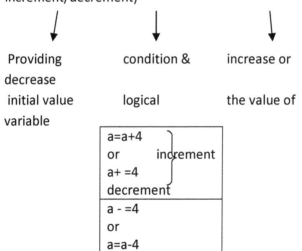

Providing decrease	condition &	increase or
initial value	logical	the value of
variable		

| a=a+4 |
| or   increment |
| a+ =4 |
| decrement |
| a - =4 |
| or |
| a=a-4 |

1. Wrie a C program to display first ten natural numbers.

    Sol.

C-Series #1

```
void main ()
int a=1;
printf("%d",a);
for(a=1;a<=10;a++);
a++;
{
printf("%d",a;);
printf("%d",a);
 printf("\n %d",a);
a++;
}
vertical output
printf("%d",a);
}
("%d",a);
a++;
printf("%d",a);
a++;
:
;
a++;
printf("%d",a);
}
```

2. **Write a C program to print in Odd numbers.**
   Sol.
```
#include<stdio.h>
#include<conio.h>
void main ()
{
int a=1, n;
```

C-Series #1

```
clrscr();
printf("\n enter the range=");
scanf("%d",&n);
//if(a%2==0) then output even numbers
for(a=1; a<=n; a++)
{
if(a%2==1)
printf("%d",a);
}
getch();
}
```

Note: when,

3. **Write a C program to print 'n' even numbers.**

   Sol.

```
#include<stdio.h>
#include<conio.h>
void main ()
{
int a=, n;
clrscr()
printf("\n enter the range");
scanf("%d",&n);
for(a=2; a<=n; a=a+2)
{
printf("%d",a);
}
getch();
}
```

4. **Write a C program to find the sum of 'n' natural number.**

C-Series #1

Sol.
```
#include<stdio.h>
#include<conio.h>
void main ()
{
int a=1, n, sum=0;
clrscr();
printf("\n enter the range");
scanf("%d",&n);
for(a=1; a<=n;a++)
{
sum=sum+a;
}
printf("\n sum=%d",sum);
getch();
}
```

5. **Write a C program to find factorial of a number.**

Sol.
```
#include<stdio.h>
#include<conio.h>
void main ()
{
int a=1, n, fact=1;
clrscr();
printf("\n enter the number=");
scanf("%d",&n);
for(a=1; a<=n; a++)
{
fact=fact*a;
}
```

```
printf("\nfact=%d",fact);
getch();
}
```

Note:

n, for(a=n; a>0;a--)

{

Fact=fact*a;

}

6. **Write a C program to solve the series:**

$$1. \quad (1+\frac{1}{2}+\frac{1}{3}+ \text{.......} +\frac{1}{n})$$

Sol.

```
#include<stdio.h>
#include<conio.h>
Void main ()
{
Int a=1, n, sum=0;
Printf("\n enter the range");
Sacnf("%d",&n);
For(a=1; a<=n; a++)
{
Sum=sum+(||a)
}
Printf("\n sum=%d",sum);
Getch();
}
```

$$2. \quad (1^1+2^2+2^3+ \text{......} + n^n)$$

Sol.

#include<stdio.h>

C-Series #1

```c
#include<conio.h>
void main ()
{
int a=1, n, sum=0;
clrscr();
printf("\n enter the range");
scanf("%d"&n);
for(a=1; a<=n; a++)
{
sum=sum+pow(a, a);
}
printf("\n sum=%d",sum);
getch();
}
```

Q. What is nested for loop?

Ans: Nested for loop refers to the block of statement where loop lies within another loop. This is also known by nested for loop or nested for statement.

Syntax:-

```
for (i=0; i<n; i++)
{
i<3;  i++)
for (j=0;j<n; j++)
{
j<3; j++)
Statement;
}

;
```

e.g.
```
for(i=0;

{
for(j=0;
i=row
{

statement

}
```

j=c

C-Series #1

1. Write a C program to create a multiplication table from 1 o 5.

Sol.

```
#include<stdio.h>
#include<conio.h>
void main ()
{
int i, j;
for (i=1; i<5; i++)
{
for (j=1;j<10; j++)
{
printf("\n %dx%d=%d",i,j(i*j));
}
}
getch();
}
```

2. Write a C program to compute the f^n $z = 3x^2 + 2y^3 - 25.5$, where x varies from -1.5 to 1.5 in increments of 0.5 and y varies from 0 to 5 in step of 1.

Sol.

```
#include<stdio.h>
#include<conio.h>
void main ()
{
float z, x, y;
for(n= - 1.5; n<=1.5; x=x+0.5)
{
for(y=0; y,3; y++)
{
```

C-Series #1

```
z=(3*x*x)+(2*y*y*y*y) – 25.5;
printf("\n z=%f",z);
}
}
getch();
}
```

Q. Define while loop and do…while () loop, Differentiate between for loop, while loop and do…while () loop.

Ans: A while loop is used to execute and repeat a block of statements depending on a condition. The syntax for while loop.

Syntax:

```
I=initialization
While (condition)
{
Statement;
Increment/decrement;
}
```

A do…while loop is used to execute and repeat a block of statements depending upon a condition

Syntax:-

```
i=initialization;
{
Statement;
Increment/decrement;
}
While (condition);
```

For	While	Do…while
(i) A for loop is	(i) A while loop	(i) A do…while ()

used to execute repeat a statement block depending on a condition which is evaluated at the beginning of the loop.	is used to execute and repeat a statement block depending on a condition which is evaluated at the beginning of the loop.	loop is used to execute and repeat a statement block depending on a condition which is executed at the end of the loop.
(ii) A variable value is initialized at the beginning of the loop and is used in the condition.	(ii) A variable value is initialized at the beginning or before the loop and is used in the condition.	(ii) A variable value is initialized before the loop or assign inside the loop and is used in the condition.
(iii) A statement to change the value of the condition or to increment the value of the variable is given at the beginning of the loop.	(iii) A statement to change the value of the condition or to increment the value of the variable is given inside the loop.	(iii) A statement to change the value of the condition or to increment the value of the variable is given inside the loop.
(iv) The statement block will not be executed when the value of the condition is false	(iv) The statement block will not be executed when the value of the condition is false.	(iv) The statement block will not be executed when the value of the condition is false, but the block is

C-Series #1

		executed at least once irrespective of the value of the condition.
(v) A for loop is commonly used by many programs	(v) A while loop is also widely used by many programs.	(v) A do...while () loop is used in some cases where the condition need to be checked at the end of the loop.

1. Write a C program to display first ten natural number using while loop.

   Sol.
   ```
   #include<stdio.h>
   #include<conio.h>
   void main ()
   {
   int a;
   a=1; //initialization
   while (a<=10) //condition
   {
   printf("\n %d",a); //output
   a++; //increment
   }
   getch();
   }
   ```
2. Write a C program to print 'n' odd number using while loop.

C-Series #1

Sol.
```
#include<stdio.h>
#include<conio.h>
void main ()
{
int a, b;
printf("\n enter the range=");
scanf("%d",a);
a=1; //initialized
while (a<=n) //condition
{
printf("\n%d",a);
a=a+2; // incerement
}
getch();
}
```
*Note: for, while loop never terminates only do while loop terminates i.e. while or pare no colon.

3. **Write a C program to find the factorial of a number using while loop.**

Sol.

| ```
#include<stdio.h>
#include<conio.h>
void main ()
{
int i, num, fact=1;
printf("\n enter any number=");
scanf("%d",&num);
i=1;
while(i<=num)
``` | Fact=1*(i=1)<br>Fact=1<br>Fact=1*(i=2)<br>Fact=2<br>Fact=2*(i=3)<br>Fact=6<br>Fact=6*(i=4)<br>Fact=6*4=24<br>Fact=24*(i=5)<br>Fact=24*5<br>=120 |
|---|---|
```

```
{
fact=fact*i;
i++;
}
printf("\n factorial=%d",fact);
getch();
}
```

4. **Write a C program find the factorial of a number using do...while () loop.**

   Sol.

```
#include<stdio.h>
#include<conio.h>
void main ()
{
int i, num, fact=1;
printf("\n enter any number");
scanf("%d",&num);
i=1;
do
{
fact=fact*i;
i++;
}
while(i<=n);
print("\n factorial=%d,fact);
getch();
}
```

*note:
```
Do
{
D=n%10;
Rev=rev*1-
+d;
N=n/10;
}
While(n>0);
```

5. **Write a C program to reverse the number.**

   Sol.

```
#include<stdio.h>
```

C-Series #1

```c
#include<conio.h>
void main ()
{
int n, rev=0, d;
printf("\n enter any number");
scanf("%d",&n);
while(n>0)
{
d=n%10;
rev=rev*10+d;
n=n/10;
}
printf("\n reverse=%d",rev);
getch();
}
```

n=1234
d=1234%10
d=4
rev=rev*10+4=4
n=1234/10=123(4 is under float)
n=123
d=123%10=3
rev=rev*10+3=43
n=n/10=12
d=12%10=2
rev=rev*10+d
    =43*12+2=432
n=n/10=12/10=1
d=1%10
  =1

rev=rev*10+d

=432*10+1

=4321

n=1/10

n=0(now, n) 0, not possible

6. **Write a C program to check whether the number is palindrome or not.**

   Sol.

```
#include<stdio.h>
#include<conio.h>
void main ()
{
int n, rev=0, d, temp;
printf("\n enter any number");
scanf("%d",&n);
temp=n;
while(n>0)
{
d=n%10;
rev=rev*10+d;
n=n/10;
}
if(temp==rev)
{
printf("\n number is palindrome=");
}
else
{
printf("\n number is not palindrome=");
}
```

*note:

Using do...while ()

```
Do
{
D=n%10;
Rev=rev*10+d;
N=n/10;
}
While(n>0);
```

121 is palindrome

123 is not

```
getch();
}
```

7. **Write a C program to find the sum of a digit of a number.**

Sol.

Using while loop:

```
#include<stdio.h>
#include<conio.h>
void main ()
{
int sum, num, digit;
sum=0; //initialization of variable
prinf("\n enter any number =");
scanf("%d",num);
while (num>0)
{
digit=num%10;
sum=sum+digit;
num=num/10;
}
printf("\n sum=%d",sum);
getch();
}
```

Sol.

Using do...while () loop.

```
#include<stdio.h>
#include<conio.h>
void main ()
{
int sum, num, digit;
```

```
sum=0; //initialization of variable
prinf("\n enter any number =");
scanf("%d",num);
do
{
digit=num%10;
sum=sum+digit;
num=num>10;
}
while(num>0)
printf("\n sum=%d",sum)
getch();
}
```

e.g.

Act, num=123

Digit=num%10=123%10=3(reminder)

Sum=sum+digit=0=3=3

num=num/10=123/10=12.3=12

$\overline{\text{digit}=12\%10=2}$

sum=3+2=5

num=sum/10=12/10=1.2=1

$\overline{\text{digit}=1\%10=1(1 \text{ is not divisible by } 10)}$

sum=5+1=6

num=num/10=1/10=0.1=0(condition false(num>0) loop stoped)

8. **Write a C program to check whether the number is prime or not.**

Sol.

```
#include<stdio.h>
#include<conio.h>
```

```
void main ()
{
int num, fae, i;
printf("\n enter the number to check prime
possibility=");
sacnf("%d",&num");
fae=0;
for(i=1; i<=num; i++)
{
if (num%i=0)
}
}
if(fae==2)
printf("\n this is prime number=");
else
printf("\nthis is not a prime number=");
getch();
}
```

The above program written in another process:

```
#include<stdio.h>
#include<conio.h>
void main()
{
int num, i, x=0, ren, mid;
printf("\n enter any number");
sacnf("%d",&num);
mid=num/2;  //find mid value
for(i=2; i<=mid && x==0; i++)
{
ren=num%i
if(ren=0)
{
```

Note:

To check quality x==0 rems to check wherever equal or not & x=0 to owing a value or transfer the value 'l'Must be less than or equal to mid & also x=0 If one of the condition is false, the whole loop will be terminated.

```
x=1;
}
}
if(x==0)
printf("\n prime no=");
else
print("\n not prime number=");
getch()
}
```

3. **Write a C program to print all prime numbers up to the given limit.**

   Sol.
```
#include<stdio.h>
#include<conio.h>
void main ()
{
int num, i, j, fae=0;
printf("\n enter the range");
scanf("%d",&num);
for(i=1, i<=num; i++)
{
if (i%j==0)
{
fae=fae+1;
}
}
if (fae==2)
printf("\n%d",i);
}
getch();
}
```

C-Series #1

4. **Write a C program to find the series of fabauiui up to 'n' teem 0113458.**

   Sol.

```
#include<stdio.h>
#include<cono.h>
void main ()
{
int n1, n2, new, n;
printf("\n enter the limit of series");
sacnf("%d",&n);
n1=0;
n2=1;
printf(('\n %d%d"n1,n2);
while1(new<=n)
{
new=n1+n2;
printf("%d",new);
n1=n2;
n2=new;
}
getch();
}
```

Note:

Char a=B, b[20]=abc

Charch; - single

Character variable

Char ch[20]; -

muti character variable

ASCII value

A-Z=65-90

a-z=97-122

% remainder findings

String Manipulation

String handing function in C:

There are four important string handling function in C language:

i. Strlen ()
ii. Strcat ()
iii. Strcpy ()
iv. Strcmp ()

(i) **Strlen () (function):** Strlen () function in C language is used to calculate the number of character in a string.

e.g.
char name [20]; // string variable declearation
Int;
Scanf("%s",name);
L=strlen (name);
Printf("\n length=%d",&);

(ii) **Strcat ()** : Strcat () is used to join character strings when two character strings are joined, it is referred concatenation of string.

e.g.
char name [10];="ANTARA",little[10]="PAUL";
strcat (name, little); **{ little – source, name – destination}**

(iii) **Strcpy ()** : Strcpy () is used to copy a character string to a character variable.

e.g.
char name[10];
strcpy (name, "INDIA");

(iv) **Strcmp ():** Strcmp () is used to compare two character strings. It returns a zero when two strings are identical, otherwise it returns a numerical value which is the difference in ASCII values of the first mismatching character of the strings being compared.

e.g.
char str1 [5]="RAM", srt2[5]="ram";
strcmp(str1, str2);

Reading writing methods: Character input output function in C language for strings are categorized in two methods: -

(i) Reading strings which do not have any while spaces.

(ii) Reading string which have white space.

e.g.

char str 1[100];

printf("\n enter any words/sentence:=);

Method1:

Scanf("%s", str1); // read string without white spaces

Printf("\n name:%s",na,e);

Method1	Method2
Antara Paul	Antara Paul
Name: Antata	Name: Antara Paul

Writing functions:

e.g.

char str[100];

printf("\n enter any word/sentence:");

Method – 1

Scanf("%s",str1); // Read string without white spaces – input

Printf("\n name:%d", name); - output

└──→ This is the first method of writing

Method – 2

Gets (str1); - input

Printf("\n name");

Puts(str1); - output

└──→ This is the second method of writing.

Additional string handling function:

C-Series #1

The following string handling function which are formed within two heads tiles –

#include<sting.h>
#include<ctype.h>
#include<stdlib.h>

String – gr, of character
Ctype- character
Stdlib – standard library

a. **Strupr ():** This type is used o convert all alphabets in a string to upper case letters.
   Ex.
   Str[s]= "hello"
   Strupr(str)= HELLO;

b. **Strluer ():** This function is used to convert all alphabets in a string to lower case letters.
   Ex.
   Str[s]="HELLO";
   Strluer[str]=hello;

c. **Str rev ():** This function is used to reverse the contents in a string.
   Ex.
   Str[s]="hello";
   Str rev(str)=olleh;

d. **Strncmp ():** This function is used to compare the first 'n' character of two strings.
   Ex.
     Strncmp("DELHI",DIDAR",2);
        4   4   5   9   IE – 5, 1 – 9, 9 –
   4
          | | | A –
   1
          D   D   E   I

O(diff)   -4(diff)

e. **Strcmpi ():** This function is used to compare two string s with case insensitive neglecting lower and upper case.

Ex.
Strcmpi("delhi","DELHI");

f. **Strncat():** This function is used to join specific number of letters to another string.

e.g.

str1[5]="new"
str2[5]="Delhi"
strncat(str1, str2, 3);
output= New del

1. **Write a C program to compare the length of a string.**
Sol.

```
#include<stdio.h>
#include<conio.h>
#include<string.h>
void main ()
{
char namr[30]
int l;
printf("\n enter any word or sentence");
gets(name);
l=strlen(name);
printf("\n length of string=%d",l);
```

```
getch();
}
```

2. **Write a C program to compare two different string.**
    Sol.
    ```
    #include<stdio.h>
    #include<conio.h>
    #inclucde<string.h>
    void main ()
    {
    char name[30], name 1[30];
    printf("\n enter two word or sentence");
    gets(name);
    gets(name1);
    if(strcmp(name, name1)==0)
    printf("\n strings are equal");
    else
    printf("\n strings are net equal");
    getch();
    }
    ```

3. **Write a C program to copy a string from one string**
    variables to another string variable.
    Sol.
    ```
    #include<stdio.h>
    #include<conio.h>
    #inclucde<string.h>
    void main ()
    {
    char name[30], name1[30];
    printf("\n enter any word or sentence");
    gets(name);
    stecpy(name1, name);
    ```

    > **Note:**
    > Or instead
    > of puts we
    > can as
    > prinf("\nco
    > pied
    > string;%s",
    > name(1);

```
    printf("\n copied string")
    puts(namr1);
    getch();
    }
```

4. **Write a C program to join different sting variable.**
   Sol.
   ```
   #include<stdio.h>
   #include<conio.h>
   #include<string.h>
   void main ()
   {
   char name [30], name1 [30];
   printf("\n enter a word or sentence");
   gets(name);            e.g – hello
   gets(name1);            – world
   strcat (name, name1); //if join 'name1' after 'name'
   or
   strear(name1, name); //if join 'name' after 'name1'
   printf("\n after concatenation=");
   puts(name1);
   puts(name);
   getch();
   }
   ```

5. **Write a C program to count the number of variables and consonants.**
   Sol.
   ```
   #include<stdio.h>
   #include<conio.h>
   #include<string.h>
   ```

C-Series #1

```
void main ()
{
char name [300];
int vow=0, con=0, i, l, sp=o;
printf("\n enter any scentance");
gets(name);
l=strcten(name);
for (i=0; i<l; i++)
{
Case'A':
Case'E':
Case'I':
Case'O':
Case'U':
Case'a':
Case'e':
Case'i':
Case'o':
Case'u':
vow++
break;
case' ':
spa++;
}
}
con=l-vow-sp;
printf("\n no of vowels=%d",vow);
printf("\nno of consonants=%d",con);
getch();
}
```

6. **Write a C program to count the number of words and spaces in a sentence.**
   Sol.

```c
#include<stdio.h>
#include<conio.h>
#include<string.h>
void main ()
{
char name[300];
int wd=0, sp=0, i, l;
printf("\n enter any sentence");
gets(name);
l=strlen(name);
for(i=0; i<l; i++)
{
if (name[i]==' ')
sp++;
}
wd=sp++;
printf("\nno of space=%d",sp);
printf("\n no of word=%d",wd);
getch();
}
```

ABOUT MY VIEW

This book is about the basic knowledge on C Language. By giving respect to Dennis Ritchie i Debajyoti Bhattacharjee by self publish this book to create a basic programming approach towards the society. My work is to make everybody eligible for programming language. This is my first series of C book. The contains various approaches regarding string, loops, matrix, file system, graphics etc.

Thanks For Your Little Support...
From,
Debajyoti Bhattacharjee